LITTLE OAK
LEARNS A BIG LESSON

WRITTEN BY
SHELIA ROCCHIO

ILLUSTRATED BY
NICKIE ROCCHIO

Copyright ©2023 Shelia Rocchio

Written by Shelia Rocchio
Illustrated by Nickie Rocchio

Published by Miriam Laundry Publishing Company
miriamlaundry.com

All rights reserved. This book or any portion thereof may not be reproduced or used in any manner whatsoever without the express written permission from the author except for the use of brief quotations in a book review.

Florence, CO
Library of Congress Control Number: 2023903306

HC ISBN 978-1-998816-41-5
PB ISBN 978-1-998816-40-8
e-Book ISBN 978-1-998816-39-2

FIRST EDITION

To you holding this book,
when things don't work out as you had planned, may you have the courage to keep growing and remember it is part of your beautiful story!

Thank you to everyone who has supported me on this journey. I am extremely grateful!

Shelia

A special thank you to my son Nickie,
for bringing this story to life with your beautiful illustrations.

One day the children went with Momma and Daddy to a plant nursery to buy a new tree. They looked at plum trees and maple trees and birch trees. Then they saw Little Oak.

"This tree is perfect!" exclaimed the children.

Momma and Daddy looked it over. "Oh yes, it is!"

The family took the little tree home and planted it in the center of the yard. They watered and fertilized it, and the little tree felt happy and special. Its roots were no longer cramped in a planter and had room to stretch and grow in the ground. It felt good!

The little tree was welcomed by all the friendly backyard buddies. There were trees, shrubs, flowers, squirrels, birds, frogs, lizards, butterflies, and ladybugs. The yard was such a beautiful place!

The family showed the little tree kindness and care over the next couple of years as it grew and grew and became sturdy and strong. The children loved to play around it.

The little tree felt needed and loved in its backyard home.

It held bird nests in its branches early in the spring.

It provided shade for the children and pets in the hot summer sun.

In the fall, the squirrels loved to climb and play in the tree's brightly colored branches.

When winter came its branches held feeders for the hungry birds.

The little tree loved its home with the family and its backyard buddies.

It dreamed of growing even **BIGGER, TALLER** and **STRONGER** like other trees in the yard and neighborhood!

It would be a **MIGHTY** oak!

Then one year something unusual happened...

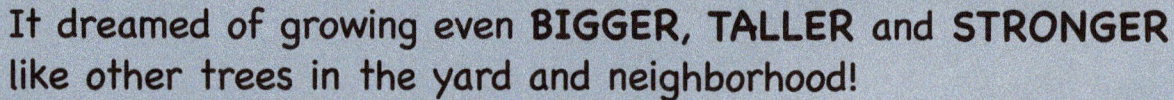

Late one night, in September, it got very cold, and it started to snow!

It snowed and snowed all night.

The little tree hadn't dropped its leaves yet, and now snow lay thick and heavy on each leaf. The little tree moaned with the weight on its branches.

"Oh no!" said Momma when she woke up the next morning. "It snowed last night!"

It was not winter yet.

It was September and snow usually came in late October or November.

Momma went outside. Everything was covered with snow and ice!

Then she saw it ... the poor little tree had broken! The weight of the snow had broken a branch and cracked it completely off!

Momma and Daddy brushed the heavy snow off the tree and repaired it the best they could.

Oh, how they hoped it would be okay. They would have to wait until spring to see if it would have buds.

Would Little Oak survive the cold winter months ahead?

As spring drew closer, the children watched and waited to see if the tree would get buds. They watched and waited and watched and waited.

And then...

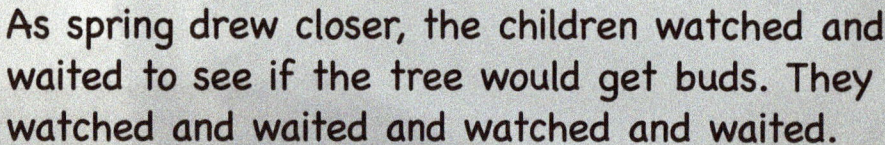

"Buds!" they exclaimed. The little tree would be okay but would never look the same.

Over the spring and summer, the little oak continued to grow but didn't like itself.

I'm ugly, scarred and look funny compared to the other trees!
What good am I now?
What will others think of me?
Why did this have to happen to me?

It grew more unhappy and complained every day.

One day a little bluebird landed on the tree. "Why do you look so sad?"

"I look funny," grumbled the tree. "I am missing a big branch."

"You don't look funny. Lots of trees are damaged in storms. It's a badge of courage that you survived," tweeted the bluebird as he ate from the birdfeeder. "That's what Momma bird told me when I hurt my wing and got a scar from Mrs. Jones' cat. It's my badge of courage!"

Birdseed spilled out of the bluebird's beak. "Momma also says not to talk with food in my mouth."

He and the tree laughed together.

The little bird continued, "You went through a bad storm and are still standing!"

The little tree thought for a moment.

"You're right! I am still standing and have a lot to be happy for!
I can still provide shade on hot sunny days.
I can still hold bird nests and feeders.
I have beautiful colored leaves in the fall.
Who knows what I will do as I grow and grow!"

"That's the spirit!" exclaimed the little bluebird as he flew away from the tree. "See you later!"

The little tree watched as the little bluebird splashed and told jokes at the birdbath.

Little Oak realized that a scarred wing didn't keep the bluebird from bringing joy and happiness to others in the backyard.

It stopped thinking about its broken branch and no longer compared itself to others.

Instead, it kept doing its job — sheltering birds, providing shade, and dazzling with color. The little oak tree and bluebird became very good friends.

Then one day, something really exciting happened!

Daddy and Momma had a surprise.

Because the oak tree had lost a branch, it had the perfect space for a tree fort!

After it was built, the children loved to climb up and spend hours playing, talking, reading, and laughing in the fort.

When friends and family came to visit, the favorite thing for all the children to do was play in the tree fort together.

The oak tree loved listening to the children and having them in its branches.

"I love this oak tree!" said the little girl. "I'm glad it survived that bad storm."

"Yes, it's the best tree ever with the coolest tree fort ever!" said the little boy.

As the oak tree listened, it felt grateful for its backyard home and the branch it lost.

Little Oak realized that it had become a **MIGHTY** oak after all.

ABOUT THE AUTHOR

Shelia Rocchio lives in Colorado with her husband. She has three grown sons, two daughters-in-law and two grandchildren. Shelia loves to spend time with her family, read, write, paint, garden and take vacations by the beach, where she can snorkel. Shelia has over twenty years' experience in Early Childhood and Elementary Education. She is a Certified Life Coach for both adults and children and loves to inspire others to see both the good around them and within them. She is the author of the bestselling children's book *Toby the Turtle*. You can learn more about Shelia, find her books and receive free resources on her website, www.sheliarocchio.com.

ABOUT THE ILLUSTRATOR

Nick Rocchio has loved drawing since he was a young boy. He graduated from the Academy of Art University in San Francisco with a degree in Computer Animation. His art practice includes drawing, painting, graphic design and illustration. He is the illustrator of the bestselling children's book *Toby the Turtle*. Nick is an avid outdoorsman. In his spare time, you can find him fishing, hunting, hiking and camping in the beautiful state of Washington, where he happily resides with his wife and young daughter. You can find samples of his artwork and learn more about him at his website, www.nickrocchio.com.

Printed in the USA
CPSIA information can be obtained
at www.ICGtesting.com
LVHW070600260823
756371LV00001B/1